Ghosts: A Message From The Illuminati

by Dr. Alexander J. McIvor-Tyndall

with an introduction by "Black Books"

COVER CREDITS

Front Cover
Anti-New World Order by VOCSociety (Own work)
[CC BY-SA 4.0 (https://creativecommons.org/licenses/by-sa/4.0)],
via Wikimedia Commons

Brick Walls by Rfc1394, via Open Clip Art
www.OpenClipArt.org

Cool Sunburst by revzach, via Open Clip Art
www.OpenClipArt.org

Back Cover
Photograph : Cremation of Care Ceremony, Bohemian Grove, 1907
from *The Bohemian Jinks: A Treatise* (1908)], page 94
by Gabriel Moulin

All-Seeing Eye
Public Domain Image

Black Books Logo
Candle Collection by VectorPocket, via FreePik.com
Vanitas [Painting] by Bartholomäus Bruyn the Elder, Public Domain
Marbled Pedestal with Old Books by Kues1, via FreePik.com

Fonts
Diehl Deco and *Attentica 4F* by Apostrophic Labs, via Da Font
www.DaFont.com

Research / Sources
Wikimedia Commons
www.Commons.Wikimedia.org

Many thanks to all the incredible photographers, artists,
researchers, and archivists who share their great work.

PLEASE NOTE :
As with all reprinted books of this age that are intended to perfectly reproduce the original edition,
considerable pains and effort had to be undertaken to correct fading and sometimes outright damage to
existing proofs of this title. At times, this task can be quite monumental, requiring an almost total
rebuilding of some pages from digital proofs of multiple copies. Despite this, imperfections still sometimes
exist in the final proof and may detract slightly from the visual appearance of the text.

DISCLAIMER :
Due to the age of this book, some methods or practices may have been deemed unsafe or unacceptable in
the interim years. In utilizing the information herein, you do so at your own risk. We republish antiquarian
books without judgment or revisionism, solely for their historical and cultural importance, and for
educational purposes.

Introduction

$\mathcal{B}$*lack* $\mathcal{B}$*ooks* are so excited to bring you a special reprint edition of the rare old book.

Firstly, ***Ghosts : A Message from the Illuminati*** is <u>*NOT*</u> about ghosts! Not the paranormal sort, anyway.

The Illuminati are the cabal that rules the world. They are the invisible government that none of us know, none of us see, those who run our lives. Sure, we know who the Rockefellers and the Rothschilds are, and we've all heard of Financial Terrorist, George Soros, etc., but these are just the *Renfields*. These are the helpers and enablers, the public face of the *Global Elite*, or *The Illuminati*. But the upper echelons of this group, the Draculas - we will never know who they are.

This old book, written by Dr. Alexander J. McIvor-Tyndall, and first published in 1906, is fascinating in both its heart and coldness, if such diametrical opposition can exist in the same mind at the same time. Our best description of this book is, think - written equivalent of a Bohemian Grove *Cremation of Care* ceremony.

The *ghosts* McIvor-Tyndall is discussing are the things he perceives that hold a person back, stifle him in his goals and keep him from them, they are the things that fill us with fear, make us doubt. The ghosts are *Duty, Customs, Economy, Morals, Respectability*, and *Tradition*. His precept is that everything *"negative is a ghost,"* and that *"only positive things contain life."*

This book is a wonderfully contradictory read; it is written with compassion for people, is inspiring, but tells us to rid ourselves of things like duty and morals and respectability – some of the virtues that make our society tolerable to live in.

This rare old book is a must-read for all those interested in everything from social constructs to the psychology of the Global Elite.

~ $\mathcal{B}$*lack* $\mathcal{B}$*ooks*

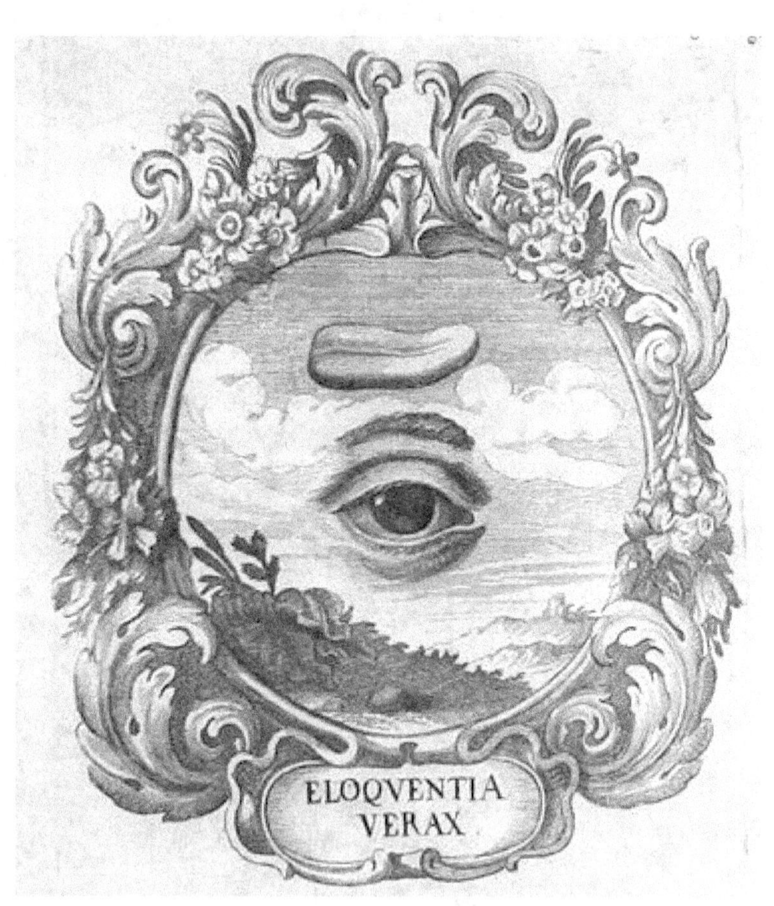
ELOQVENTIA
VERAX

The world is peopled with ghosts.

—*Henrik Ibsen.*

GHOSTS.

 AM going to tell you something about "ghosts."

Not the wraiths of the dead, whose restless souls are "doomed for a certain time to walk the earth"—like the ghost of Hamlet's father. Not the astral forms that are said to haunt deserted houses and unregenerate spots.

These are problems which Psychic Research has partially fathomed, and which will in time be thoroughly clear to human understanding.

I am going to tell you of the ghosts one meets every day in this practical, commercial age.

The ghosts that shake hands with you, as it were, in business and social intercourse.

The ghosts that influence your every act, that affect your every thought, and determine your every spoken word.

I am going to discover to your notice the ghosts of dead ideas; of lifeless customs; of worn out ethics; of unconsidered codes of morals, and unfollowed rules of conduct—of all the accumulation of false concepts of the ages, which we have named *Tradition*.

Ibsen, the great Norwegian psychologist, treats of these dead ideas, in his dramas, particularly, perhaps, in the powerful and fascinating play called "Ghosts."

The "great man of Norway" is an iconoclast.

He represents to the drama in a measure what the late Robert Ingersoll represented in the religious thought of the last century.

Ibsen alludes to the artificial ideas and customs which have held sway over the lives of people throughout generations—as "ghosts."

And he portrays most interestingly and dramatically, the manner in which the world is tyrannized over by these non-vital beliefs and conventionalities.

Ibsen is a great preacher.

His plays are powerful sermons.

In the drama "Ghosts" he depicts the result upon human character of a life of repression; of deceit; of compulsory observation of the false concepts that have stood to human conduct for morals.

There are those who call Ibsen's plays immoral.

This view of the dramatic sermons of the great psychologist, is the result of superficial observation.

Ibsen compels intelligent analysis.

Apart from their intensely fascinating and dramatic situations, Ibsen's dramas are built upon the deepest knowledge of psychological research. Naturally, to the superficial observer, who sees only the dramatic *effect,* the *lesson,* the *sermon,* in fact, preached so powerfully in "Ghosts," fails in mission, because he sees only the fascination of the play itself.

It requires the subtleness of the analytical mind to fathom the depth of meaning in the lines, because the meaning is essentially psychological.

Unfortunately, the world is made up largely of superficial observers. We are but now beginning to look below the surface of things.

The average mind sees only the *effect,* and fails to penetrate the *cause.*

Psychology is a science that teaches us to look below the surface—to seek the *soul* of things—to reason from *effect* to *cause,* as well as from *cause* to *effect.*

And we are glad to observe that the study of psychology is becoming almost general.

Indeed, psychology is now fashionable, and let us hope that out of the illusion of fashion, something of permanent good may come.

✓ ✓ ✓

IN the study of psychology, we have recently passed through an age of phenomena.

Phenomena are reflections—surface results.

Psychic phenomena are the caps

upon the psychic wave that is at present engulfing the entire world.

Phenomena serve to show us the substance beneath.

They attract our attenton to the facts underlying their production.

The phenomena are important only as they disclose the law of which they are a result. And in order to make people see below the surface—the phenomena—it is sometimes necessary to employ drastic measures.

We are apt to jog along in the narrow path blazed for us by former generations, without apprehending the necessity for accommodating ourselves to a wider perspective, a larger viewpoint, than was possible to our ancestors.

Ibsen recognizes this fact, and seeks to awaken the public mind, by fearlessly exposing its narrowness.

Ibsen has been called a pessimist, because of his powerful portrayal of the morbid character of Oswald in "Ghosts."

Oswald, you will remember is the result of a loveless marriage between a woman of strong mentality and a dissolute man, whose excesses and dissipations were concealed in deference to society and the church.

Naturally, the child of such a union could not be a healthy, normal one.

And Ibsen follows this logical conclusion to the extreme point.

He makes the child of this union, Oswald, a mental wreck, and thereby enters a protest against all that is not honest, vital and natural.

Ibsen may be considered a moral surgeon.

He desires to open the wilfully

closed eyes of the world, and to teach the world that disease is mental and moral, as well as physical.

Every word he puts into the mouths of his characters conveys this message.

Every phrase, every situation, is psychological in depth—purposeful in effect.

But Ibsen is not a pessimist.

His object is quite sufficiently optimistic.

The iconoclast who tears aside the veil from a condition he desires to make better, may have the most auspicious motive.

Ingersoll, for example, led the life of a consistent Christian, while protesting with all the eloquence with which he was endowed, against the shams and hypocricies that often prevail under the name of "Christianity." So with Ibsen.

His evident object is to convey the message that social pretense, rigid discipline, and the narrow view taken of life by many so-called religious people, are empty forms and hypocritical pretenses.

And he goes on to demonstrate that these hypocricies, harbored in the mind, and lived from generation to generation, result inevitably, in *degeneration*.

He chose the title "Ghosts" for his dramatic sermon, because from the metaphysical viewpoint, the "ghost" represents the empty shell of the physical body after the vitality—the soul—has left it.

He shows the analogy between these "ghosts," and worn out creeds, unwritten and unobserved laws and all the ethics that were established at a time when human intellect was not considered trustworthy.

Psychically speaking, "ghosts" are not living entities, as are what are often called "spirits."

Ghosts are non-vital—empty—something that our imagination inspires with temporary power.

When, as occurs in the drama we are discussing, Ibsen speaks of "the world being peopled with ghosts," he means that the world is filled with unhealthy, non-vital ideas, thought creations of the carnal mind, that have no place or part in the operation of that which is lasting, eternal and true.

One of these world-ghosts is the prevalent idea that work is a curse. That labor is something of which to be ashamed—something to be avoided when possible, and at whatever cost.

 NOTHER "world-ghost" is that it is our duty to suffer—that life is not meant to be happy and full of the joy of living.

That we are to undergo trials and tribulations and hardships on earth in order that we may enter a place called "Heaven"—sometime in the intangible future.

Another ghost that haunts us all and makes slaves of us, is the ghost of conventionality—than which nothing could be more lifeless.

Concealment, affectation, pretensions that are absurd on the face of them, are ghosts that master us, control our every moment—and reduce us to abject slavery.

Duty; Economy; Respectability; are synonyms for "ghost."

They are inherited thought concepts—man-made fences, that keep us from entering into "green fields and pastures new."

I know that this will seem almost sacrilegious to many of my readers.

Duty! why the word has been made almost sacred!

It has been surrounded by a halo, and the halo has dazzled our eyes, until we have become hypnotized into accepting the word, as a commandment of the Most High.

The duty children owe their parents; the duty of wives to their husbands and of husbands to their wives; the duty we owe our country; the duty we owe society; and the thousand and one other duties that we are enjoined to observe from infancy to old age.

They are "ghosts," every one of them. No service that is not actuated by love—voluntarily and freely offered—is worth having.

Children owe nothing to their parents if those parents cannot command voluntary respect by their own force of character.

Duty to one's country is the ghost above all others that haunts and frightens humankind.

It makes men kill each other and engenders hate in children yet unborn.

Because of the ghost of duty to one's country, we see rulers of great nations sitting upon gem-studded thrones and playing the game of war with human lives as puppets.

Don't believe the fallacy.

You owe your country nothing.

Your country owes you everything.

If it fail in the fulfillment of that debt, you owe it to yourself to seek a wiser and better country.

The recognition of this truth has made America.

It is this perception that constitutes the difference between an absolute monarchy and a republic.

The imperial form of government says "The country and the country's ruler are of major importance."

"The people are the servants—the slaves, if need be—of His Majesty."

In a republic the government head, is the servant of the people. The rights of the individual are paramount.

Support of such a government is not allied to what we know as "duty."

It is not duty but wisdom that bids us conserve the interests of such a country.

ET us consider the "duty" one owes society.

That duty is to preserve at all costs, the conventionalities.

In other words, your outward life shall be such as to cause no comment —no criticism.

With your inner life society does not concern itself, and therefore, if "concealment like a worm," destroy all that is good within your mind, society does not care. You shall have done your "duty."

Don't trouble your head about society.

Again I say, you owe it nothing.

All that you owe, you owe to *yourself*.

Shakespeare, the Illumined, said:

"This above all: to thine own self be
　　　true
And it must follow, as the night the day,
Thou canst not then be false to any
　　　man."

If each person in this vast Universe
would but *realize* this truth, and live
it, we would soon "lay" these haunt-
ing, staring, fear-compelling ghosts
with which, as Ibsen says, "the world is
peopled."

But few there are who dare to face
the truth.

Fear, the prolific parent of all the
brood of ghosts, chills the blood, and
paralyzes the reason.

We dare not face the truth, and we
go on hiding our real thoughts, and
pretending to believe that the dead

ideas handed down to us by dead men, are living precepts by which to mould our conduct, so as to *finally* reach that which is desirable.

We forget that that which is always in the future is never ours.

We find in histories of superstition; in psychical literature; and in our own experience, that people are frequently frightened into insensibility by alleged "ghosts," which, on investigation, proved to be the shadow of a tree, a rock, or the effect of moonlight.

Nevertheless, the shadow, mistaken for reality, has been sufficient to produce death.

Consider for a moment the old idea of a hell of eternal punishment.

How long it held sway over the minds of men, who dared not challenge its right to acceptance.

But when the time came, that the barbarous thought-concept was thoroughly looked into and compared with our maturer experience, it vanished, as completely as the ghostly shadow of the rock in the light of day.

Ghosts cannot withstand the light.

No one ever heard of day-time ghosts.

There are spirit visitors, invisible beings, whose presence may be discerned in the day as well as in the night.

But these are realities, although invisible to mortal eye.

They are as vital as we are.

They are as different from "ghosts" as Courage is from Fear: Love from Hate: Truth from Falsehood.

The one is vital, lasting, lifegiving.

The other is a shadow, an empty thing, an illusion, that must vanish before the light of understanding as the shadows of night vanish before the rising sun.

❦ ❦ ❦

LL negative conditions are ghosts.

It is only the positive things that contain life.

Conditions cease the moment we refuse to contribute to their vitality, by our thought-force.

Hundreds of persons are frightened to death by the ghost of public opinion.

And yet, how often public opinion is founded upon a lie.

Hypocrisy is the most detestable thing in human imperfection.

Personally I have more respect for the highway robber who dares to hold up a stage coach than I have for the social pretender who thinks one thing and acts contrary to his convictions.

The former is at least demonstrating courage, though misdirected.

And courage is of itself a virtue. It is something vital, positive and possible of great results.

Worry, Doubt, Fear, Regret, and Custom are ghosts—every one of them.

Ghosts that frighten the world into powerlessness and moral death.

Who has not been able to look back upon some time of great worry, and wonder how he could have built realities out of that which did not exist?

Worry fills our world with nameless terrors that seem to us like positive entities.

In the light of Understanding they assume their proper places and we know them for mere ghosts that might have been "laid" had we but known how.

Regret is responsible for more suffering, perhaps, than any other of the ghost family.

There are sensitive beings to whom the making of a mistake, or the loss of an ideal is so terrible a thing, that they must forever go about in "sackcloth and ashes."

They live so continually in the poison of regret, that they are robbed of their vitality.

It deprives them of the power to profit by their mistakes, which is the legitimate office of mistakes.

Regret comes of teaching the fallacy of repentance and penance.

Such a doctrine is killing to all that is godlike within the human breast.

Each thought of regret is so much

waste of time and of strength and of life itself.

Regret is the grave-digger of all hope and attainment.

If we could but reach the point where we see life as a *whole,* we would perceive that all so-called mistakes are the warp that supplies the foundation for the woof of development and growth.

Whatever you have done, or may yet do, don't let the ghost of regret haunt you and deprive you of happiness and your inherent power.

No one ever profited by regretting anything.

One may learn from one's experiences.

But no one ever learned anything by holding to the thought of regret.

It is a ghost.

When you estimate it as such, it will vanish.

USTOM is another ghost that frightens most of us into trembling submission to its tyranny. We all do things, daily and hourly, not because we want to do them, nor because there is any special virtue in doing them, but because it is the "custom."

It is the custom to judge our fellow-men by their ability to make money.

Material wealth is the great illusion of the age.

Money is not wealth, however much we try to make it so.

To be wealthy (well-thy) is to be at peace with one's self, and with the world.

To be free from the hypnotic control of the idea that money is power.

Money will not purchase Wisdom, Love, Peace, or Happiness.

It will not purchase substance, however we mistake the shadow for the substance.

Wisdom alone is *power*.

Money, Custom, Fashion are mere "ghosts."

So is the belief in fate as a ruling power; the doctrine of non-responsibility of human beings; the belief that we are "miserable sinners," and "worms of the earth." As long as we believe we are spiritual worms of the earth, so long will we crawl.

It is time these ghost ideas were "laid," so that they may no longer paralyze human effort and make wrecks of human lives.

"Dignity" and "Respectability" are synonyms for "ghost."

They are dead words.

They stand too often, these times, for a long face and harsh judgment of other's acts; of outward honesty preserved at the expense of inner generosity.

Dignity! Respectability!!

There is little, indeed, in the words to appeal to the heart of a child.

And *one who knew* said: Unless ye become as little children ye cannot enter into the kingdom of Heaven," meaning *Happiness*.

Long, too long, the world has been taught the destructive, degenerating fallacy that we have no right to be happy.

Long enough shortsighted theologians have preached the doctrine of salvation through sacrifice.

It is nothing less than blasphemy to shift the responsibility of sickness and suffering and all the misery that "flesh is heir to," upon God.

Such inconsistencies are the ghost-ideas of our primitive ancestors and should be buried in the graves with their bones. The past is but a stepping stone to the present.

There is no more reason in holding to ancient conceptions of human ethics than to ancient modes of locomotion.

❦ ❦ ❦

GOD of wrath, of severe judgment, of desire for human idolatry and bended knee, and self-abasement, is the God of the cave-man.

Why let its-ghost haunt us in this twentieth century, frightening us into fetish worship?

Let us lay it for all time.

It is the work of this era to "lay" these ghosts of the race.

We propose to demonstrate the truth that God is All.

That sin is sickness and that all the "evils" of poverty and crime and disease are man-made, and being man-made, they may be dissipated by the positive power of the God, or *cosmic consciousness*.

As long as mankind looks outside himself to something remote and infinitely unreachable, for "salvation," just so long will he fail to attain the goal.

When mankind once realizes the fact that we have never been "lost," and that we have only to claim our right to all that is, then will cease all this strife and dissension.

" 'I am,' is the resurrection and the life," Jesus is reported to have said.

In those words he expressed the All of Life.

The consciousness of Being, in its completeness, is all there is.

When this shall have become to you a reality instead of an abstraction you will know that you were never born and that you can never die.

"Birth" and "Death" are relative terms.

It is because I regard Henrik Ibsen as one of the great ones of this age of Advanced Thinkers, that I have taken for the subject of my essay the title of one of his greatest plays, "Ghosts."

The world is ready for the annihilation of codes of ethics.

It is ready and eager for a happier interpretation of the gospel of "salvation."

We who believe in the Integrity of Divine Love are seeking to demonstrate the way of attainment—the way to be happy and healthy and satisfied, right here and right now, without waiting for an indefinite futurity—an elusive Heaven.

We are not promulgating any "new" creed, or seeking to establish any "new" religion.

We seek merely to bring to your consciousness a *realization* (a making real to you) of the Truth.

"And the Truth shall make you free."